SHOW UP
and
SHINE

Simple steps to boost your
confidence and charisma

Catherine Johns

Published in Chicago, IL by North Mayfair Press

ISBN: 978-0-0906187-0-0

Library of Congress Control Number 2013911417

Cover Design by Mark Ingraham, www.triggrcreative.com
Interior Book Design by www.pearcreative.ca
Illustrations by Kelly N. Fletcher, www.knfletcher.com
Edited by Lisa Phillips, www.editonica.com

For information about keynotes and coaching related to creating confidence and charisma, please go to www.ShowUpAndShineBook.com.

You can also download a complimentary audio version of the guided visualization in Chapter 6.

To Frank

because he lights my life

TABLE OF CONTENTS

INTRODUCTION

If you get all the respect you deserve and make all the money you want, you don't need to read this book.

This is a practical book about how women communicate in business. There are research papers and lengthy tomes and entire college courses devoted to the differences between men and women; you could spend a long time studying the history and philosophy of gender inequality in business and everywhere else.

You'll find a more pragmatic approach here: specific steps you can take today to change the results you're getting in your professional life. Oh, some of what you discover here will no doubt help you in the rest of life, too. But our main focus is better business communication. Because it's clear that people who project a powerful personal presence have more success and make more money.

I learned (the hard way!) that when I showed up in the world as a "nice girl," eager to please, desperate to be liked, and a little bit timid, I practically invited people to take advantage of me. And guess what? Some of those people didn't hesitate to take me up on the invitation.

When I began to come across more confidently and powerfully, people treated me much differently. Took me more seriously. Listened to me more carefully. Respected my opinions.

The same thing goes on in the business world all day long. Whether you own a business yourself or work in a corporate setting, you are constantly sending out signals that tell other people how to treat you. And they are responding.

People infer, from our physicality and our voice, how confident we are. How trustworthy we are. Even how smart and capable we are. Of course their assessment could be completely wrong. But once that first impression is made, it is tough to change. Makes sense to get it right in the first place, doesn't it?

You might think that by now, society would be past all this gender-difference stuff and we can all agree that it should be. But even today, the research shows that women in business meetings participate much less than their male colleagues. Women are evaluated, promoted, and compensated differently than men. Senior leaders in just about every industry are still overwhelmingly male. Most women have had the experience of feeling ignored or passed over or patronized at work.

You should read this book if any of this sounds like a familiar story to you. If you feel that you're not reaching your full potential. If your great ideas never quite get traction with your colleagues. If you're promoting your own business and you're just not attracting clients the way you'd like to. The way you need to.

I've seen women enhance their personal presence and

- Get promoted to executive positions
- Increase their sales dramatically
- Flourish in a brand new business
- Create new professional possibilities
- Feel exhilarated about their futures

You can do any of those things ... and more. You're about to discover how to show up and shine: how to own your space, speak from your core, and develop the confidence and charisma that will take you where you want to go.

CHAPTER ONE
What is Presence Anyway?

What do people experience when you walk into a room? It's worth thinking about because that experience is really the essence of Presence. What do others see when they look at you? What do they hear when you speak? And how do you make them feel?

For all the research on executive presence, leadership presence, stage presence, commanding presence, and professional presence, it comes down to that. Books have been written, conferences held, and workshops conducted. They all point in the same direction: Presence is about the way you look, the way you sound, and the way you behave.

Other words come up over and over when the experts discuss Presence: charisma, magnetism, authority, energy, gravitas. And the definitions can become quite circular.

It turns out that it's pretty tough to put your finger on exactly what Presence is. But people know it when they see it, hear it, and feel it. And they respond to it.

That makes one thing clear: having a powerful presence – the ability to show up and shine – doesn't happen in a vacuum. It includes making an authentic connection with the people around you.

The authenticity is important. A person can't just put on a Presence Mask and expect to have an impact on people. Real Presence is, well, real. It feels natural. But that doesn't mean it's something you're born with or not. Presence can be cultivated. A person can develop a powerful presence. You can develop a powerful presence.

Why would you want to spend the time and effort to do that? Because you want to succeed. Yes, it is that crucial.

Think of the famous people who have Presence: Bill Clinton, Katy Perry, Oprah, the Dalai Lama, there's a long list. And there are plenty of people with Presence who aren't famous, or at least they're not famous yet.

When people in a Powerful Presence workshop think of someone they know who has "it" and try to describe that person, the first thing they always say is, "She's confident." How, exactly, do they know she's confident? You'll learn about the signals of confidence as you continue reading, and you'll discover how you can convey that confidence yourself.

The Ariel Group teaches stage skills to business leaders. They say when people with Presence enter the room, "the energy level rises. You perk up, stop what you're doing, and focus on them. You expect something interesting to happen. It's as though a spotlight shines on them."

I'd say people with a powerful presence can even become the spotlight. Now that's shining. And you'll learn how to convey that charisma, too, as you read further.

Developing a powerful presence is especially important for women. The Center for Talent Innovation tells us, "Presence alone won't get you promoted, but its absence will impede your progress, especially if you're female."

Facebook COO Sheryl Sandberg famously urged women to make some changes in *Lean In: Women, Work, and the Will to Lead.* "We hold ourselves back in ways both big and small," she wrote, "by lacking self-confidence, by not raising our hands, and by pulling back when we should be leaning in."

How do you lean in, exactly? How do you step into your power? You'll find practical suggestions in the following pages. Suggestions that come from years of experience in the boys' club of the broadcasting business and a career as a communication coach.

Yes, it will take some effort to put these suggestions into practice. It will be so worth it.

Ready?

CHAPTER TWO
Prepare for Presence

Take Two (Minutes)

How are you going to show up for that client meeting, or job interview, or presentation? What kind of impression are you going to make? How is that person going to perceive you in the first few critical seconds?

You can go a long way toward creating confidence and charisma with a just little bit of pre-work. How little? About two minutes. That's right. It will take you only two minutes to measurably increase your confidence and charisma.

You'll discover how to do that shortly. But first, think about a time when you did feel confident. And it's okay if that time was a while ago. For some of us, experiences of confidence are hard to come by. But if you search your memory bank a bit, you'll come up with an occasion when you felt absolutely confident about something.

You might remember the time you were about to take a test; you knew the material cold, and you were confident you'd ace that test. Or take yourself back to a game of tennis or golf ... or tag. It doesn't really matter what the competition was. You were good at it and you went into that game completely confident that you were headed for victory. Or think of the day you won an award, a time when you were recognized for your skill or talent or contribution to a cause, and feel all over again how that acknowledgement boosted your confidence.

When you have that time in mind, whenever it was, notice what confidence feels like and pay attention to what confidence looks like to you.

Most people see that when they're confident they naturally take up more space. They stand up straight or sit up straight. Their shoulders are back and down and relaxed. And their face is relaxed too; we don't see a furrowed brow or tight lips on someone who's feeling really confident. They have a certain ease about them that we notice immediately.

That connection between confidence or command and taking up space applies across cultures. And, for that matter, it applies across species as well.

In animals, the dominant male is likely to be bigger than the others, and even more likely to *look* bigger. Think about a gorilla with his chest stuck out. Or picture the peacock with those gorgeous tail feathers fully spread out. Or even your cat. When cats want to establish that they're in charge, what do they do? They arch their back and make themselves bigger.

This is important: the non-verbal cues of confidence don't just communicate to the world around you. In fact, it may be that the most important person paying attention to your body language is ... *you*.

You can think of your non-verbal behavior as part of a feedback loop. When I feel confident, I display those confidence signals – the erect posture, the relaxed body, the voice that comes from my core. But the reverse is also true. When I send out those strong signals of confidence, I also send them inward. Then I respond to my own body language by feeling even more confident.

That means you can create confidence for yourself just by adopting the positions that demonstrate confidence.

People come at this question of confidence and charisma from all different angles. Some suggest psychotherapy aimed at eliminating old unwanted emotions and developing new, more useful feelings. Of course changing those emotions can take a very long time and a lot of hard work. But for some people, therapy is an excellent idea and the results can be transformative.

Other experts advocate changing your thoughts, perhaps using daily affirmations or meditation techniques. Or rearranging your mental pictures to create a different thought pattern. Or mentally challenging your beliefs to stimulate a new way of thinking over time. Those mental strategies can be helpful, and there are many others that people find useful.

Our focus here is a quick, practical, outside-in approach: if you change your body on the outside, those thoughts and feelings on the inside will change too.

Social psychologists have been looking into this feedback loop for a long time, gathering evidence that our physical state affects our emotional state. Facial feedback has gotten a lot of attention. Turns out it really is true that when you smile, if it's a natural, felt smile, you will feel happier.

It's kind of funny how they proved that. You know how tough it can be to get people to smile on command. How many times have you been in front of a camera, when someone said "Smile!" … and when you see the photograph later, it's clear that you didn't follow directions.

It seems that if you hold a pencil sideways in your mouth, the way many of us do … your facial muscles will approximate a natural, felt smile. It's often called a Duchenne smile, after the French neurologist who first identified it. You might try that now, and just see what happens to your face.

The research shows that people who smile (or people who hold a pencil sideways in their mouth) are more likely to feel happy.

And the reverse is also true. A University of Wisconsin study found Botox injections that interfere with frowning make individuals slower to feel anger or sadness. The feedback loop between the brain and the frown muscles is disrupted, so the intensity of the emotion is also disrupted. This is facial feedback in action: your face tells you how you feel.

So let's get back to this confidence question. Research from the Harvard Business School illustrates the impact your body language has on you.

You might know that in business schools, class participation plays a huge role in the way students are graded. People who hold back in class, no matter how bright they are, no matter how well they write papers or how thorough they are in their research projects, just don't get the kind of grades that more active students get.

And it's probably not a complete surprise to you that a Harvard professor noticed that the people who hold back in class tended to be women or men who didn't quite fit the typical business school mold.

Those students who were less likely to jump into a classroom discussion also looked different. They sat smaller. They were often hunched over, with their arms pulled in, their hands in their laps, and their head down. They tended to hold those closed, contracted postures over time.

So behavioral psychologist Amy Cuddy set out to discover whether those closed, contracted postures merely reflected a lack of confidence, or if it were possible that the closed, contracted postures also created a lack of confidence.

She and a colleague from Berkeley, Dana Carney, set up an experiment to test the effect of what they call Power Poses.

Strike a Pose

What is a Power Pose? It's an open, expansive posture.

Sitting with your feet up on a desk or table, your hands behind your head, elbows out – that's a Power Pose.

Or crossing your legs, with an ankle over the top of the other knee, with arms back in the same way, as men sometimes do in meetings – that's a Power Pose. The guy who sits like that is asserting his command of the room by taking up as much space as he possibly could while seated in a chair. (It's no wonder that women hate it when their male colleagues do that, is it?)

A standing Power Pose is leaning just slightly into a desk or table with the arms apart and the hands spread. Or – think about Wonder Woman. Feet planted, hands on hips, elbows out. Rock solid.

In the Harvard experiment, they were looking for the internal changes produced by these external postures. Of course, they could have just asked people how they felt, but a person's description of feelings is pretty subjective; it would be hard to measure and compare.

So they went with biochemistry instead. (This is science, after all.) The researchers took a saliva sample from each participant. And they measured two things: testosterone and cortisol.

Testosterone is connected to power and dominance, and again, that's true not just in humans, but in animals as well. The leader of the pack will have higher testosterone levels than the followers. And if someone who's not the leader has to, for some reason, become the leader, his testosterone levels will go up.

Just as with animals, powerful humans will be more confident, more assertive, more optimistic. They'll also be more likely to take a risk. And all those qualities are connected to testosterone.

Cortisol is produced in the adrenal gland and released in response to stress. Leaders are relaxed under pressure, right? So you'd likely see lower cortisol levels in someone who's in command.

Participants in the Harvard study believed they were part of some research about the endocrine system and the placement of electrodes on the body. But in reality, those electrodes were just a cover, providing an excuse so that people could reasonably be asked for a saliva sample.

After the sample was collected, they were told to hold one pose for a minute, switch to another and hold that for a minute.

Half of these students were directed to adopt high power poses, taking up lots of space. The other half were given instructions for low power poses: seated, with head down and arms pulled in, hands folded in their lap; or standing with their arms and legs crossed.

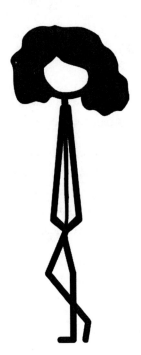

Then they had an opportunity to take a little gamble. Each person got a couple of bucks and a die; they could choose to roll the die and double their money or just hang onto their two dollars.

Next step: a follow-up saliva test.

Here's what the researchers found. In the people who adopted the high power poses ... their testosterone went up by about 20 percent. And that was true for men and women, although of course for women, their baseline for testosterone would have been lower. And for those high-power-posing people, their cortisol levels dropped by an average of 25 percent.

What about the poor people who'd been asked to hold the low power poses? Their results were just the opposite. Their testosterone went down by about 10 percent. And their cortisol levels rose by 15 percent.

Just two minutes in a high-power pose or a low-power pose literally changed their body chemistry. So based on their posture, people either moved in the direction of confidence, comfort and charisma. Or, they became more withdrawn and more reactive to stress.

The poses also influenced their willingness to take that gamble. About 60 percent of the low-power people opted to give it a go and roll the die. More like 86 percent of the people who'd been primed in a high-power pose took the opportunity to double their money.

Their bodies actually changed their minds. Your body can change your mind. It really is like flipping on your confidence switch. You can use your body to change your neuro-endocrine profile and feel more confident. And you can do it in a matter of minutes.

And it gets even better.

Power Poses were clearly demonstrated to alter body chemistry. They change how an individual feels, and they make a person more willing to take a risk. The next question was: do Power Poses actually change performance? Do other people see the results of Power-Posing without having to give you a saliva test to measure your neuro-endocrine profile?

For the second study, the researchers used something called the Trier Social Stress Test – it's a classic in the world of psychology, an experiment designed to measure psycho-social stress. It was developed at the University of Trier in Germany back in the '30's.

The TSST has been used ever since then to measure stress in response to "socially evaluative situations" which is how psychologists refer to the times and places where you're being sized up – and there are a lot of those times and places in everyone's life. I'd even argue that "socially evaluative situations" is a redundant phrase. If you're in a social situation, which is to say, there are people around … you can assume you're being evaluated. Just by looking at you those people are making judgments about how friendly you are. How confident, how honest, how competent, how intelligent and on and on. And they're making those judgments in about 7 seconds.

This is how the Harvard researchers used the Trier Social Stress Test for their Power Pose study. Imagine yourself being given five minutes to write a speech about your ideal job. You're going to convince two evaluators that you are the exact right person for this dream job, without lying about yourself.

Then you have to stand up and give the speech, using up your entire allotted time, while the evaluators sit there with their clipboards and write notes. But these evaluators are specially trained to give you no feedback. They maintain completely blank faces: no nodding, no smiling, nothing. You're just there talking about why you're the ideal candidate for this perfect job. Knowing that they're assessing you and getting no clue about what they're thinking. And as if that weren't stressful enough, there is also a video camera rolling; you're told that others will be looking at the video later and they'll be evaluating your performance too.

Makes you break out in a cold sweat just thinking about it, doesn't it? Everything about the Trier Social Stress Test is designed to create maximum stress.

So the Power Pose researchers had their participants do two minutes of high power poses before the stress test. Or two minutes of low power poses before the stress test. Then they'd go into the room where they were given their assignment and do their speeches.

The truth is that the two in-the-moment evaluators sitting there with their clipboards are really just window dressing. Like the electrodes in the first phase of the study, the evaluators aren't really doing anything. They're there to induce stress, and we can assume they're doing a pretty good job of that.

The actual evaluators, or coders, look at the video later on. They don't know who's who, they don't know anything about the hypothesis, they don't even know what's being studied. Their assignment is: look at the people on these videos. Which ones would you hire? And which ones would you reject?

You won't be surprised to hear that overwhelmingly, they looked at the high-power posers and said, "This one's great. Hire her!" And when they watched the low-power posers, their assessment was, "Forget about it. Not this one."

This is important. The difference in evaluations had nothing to do with the content of the speeches.

The difference in the evaluations was that the people who had done two minutes of high-power poses were more enthusiastic, more authentic, more confident, more comfortable, more captivating. They had presence that the low-power posers just didn't have.

That presence is the key factor that made the coders select them as the right candidates for the job.

As Amy Cuddy put it: "Our bodies change our minds. Our minds change our behavior. Our behavior changes our outcomes."

Imagine what you can accomplish when you change your outcomes, by changing your behavior, by changing your mind, by changing your body.

Remember that the Power Poses are pre-work. You wouldn't go into someone's office and stand like Wonder Woman with your hands on your hips and your chest up. You wouldn't meet with a client and sit in that I-own-the-room posture with your elbows sticking out and your hands clasped behind your head.

The idea is do these Power Poses in private before the meeting, the pitch, the interview. Power Poses are a way to prepare yourself in advance so that when you're in that stressful situation, you feel more confident, and you have a powerful presence that others will notice and respond to.

Action Steps

Write down one "socially evaluative situation" you'll be facing in the next week or so. Maybe it's standing up and introducing yourself at a networking event, making a sales presentation, or giving a toast at a wedding or retirement party. It can be anything you're going to be doing where people will be watching you, listening to you, and (whether you like it or not) evaluating you.

Figure out right now how you can use the Power Pose Strategy to prepare. How will you find a private place where you can spend two minutes in high-power poses? When will you go there? Which poses will you do? Write this plan down, too.

Make a commitment to yourself and to me that you will put Power Posing into practice now to increase your confidence and to make sure others see you as captivating and charismatic. And put that commitment in writing.

CHAPTER 3
You Must Be Present to Win

Being There

So now you know how to prepare yourself so you can project a powerful personal presence. When you start using the power poses regularly, you'll notice the difference in how people respond to you.

But presence isn't only about preparation, of course. Presence happens – hey, here's a surprise – in the present. The next chapters will show you how to make that presence happen for you.

People try all the time to think their way into confidence, and they're rarely successful. The thing about our thoughts is that they can be, and often are, occupied with the past or the future. I might be regretting something that already happened, stewing about things that didn't turn out the way I had planned, wishing I'd done something differently. Or I might be worrying about something yet to come, fretting about how it will go, and anticipating potential disaster. And I must be a time traveler;

because sometimes it seems that I can be doing both at the same time!

But my body? My body can only be right here, right now. In this place at this time. That's why the body is the perfect vehicle, perhaps the only vehicle, for getting present. And a person has to be present to have presence. You must be present to show up and shine.

So often we in Western cultures are divorced from our own bodies. Our energy is concentrated in our heads; so much so that we can completely lose touch with the rest of us. Take a moment sometime to watch people walking down a street or in a mall or at the airport. You'll see an enormous number of them walking with their heads thrust forward, all their energy concentrated in their head and neck and shoulders.

They're heading for their destination, right? They're getting ahead of themselves, in a very literal way. They're focused on what's in front of them, oblivious to the space they currently occupy, and likely disconnected from their bodies. Does that sound familiar to you? I'm a big believer that presence is developed from the ground up. It starts with your feet. So right now, wherever you are, just tune into your feet. Are they on the floor? Up on an ottoman? Maybe you have your legs crossed so one foot is flat and the other is dangling in space. Could you stand up and fly into action just as you are, without moving your feet at all? If you could, you're on your way to a powerful presence.

Of course you're reading a book right now; projecting a powerful presence isn't an issue for you at this moment.

But when it is an issue, when it matters how confident you feel, when it makes a difference how you're being perceived, you'll do well to have your feet flat on the floor, even pressing down a little bit.

In fact, try that now. Just press both feet lightly into the floor and notice that you can feel the muscles in your legs turn on. If you pay close attention, you'll experience the energy moving up and through your body. Your spine may straighten a bit more. Your shoulders relax, and the shoulder blades move down your back. Your chest is up – not sticking out, but up. Your head is straight up and down on top of your neck, your gaze straight at the horizon, so your head is neither tilted down nor up. You may feel – and you may even look – taller. It's as if you're drawing energy up from the earth; that energy is filling your body and radiating from you. You are creating a powerful presence.

This will work for you whether you're standing or seated. Either way, the energy will transform you. You don't want to look stiff or rigid, of course. Just comfortably erect, relaxed in your body, with your shoulders squared off, shoulder blades back and down – no hunching! Your chest should be open and expansive so you can breathe freely.

Now pay attention to your hands and arms. When you're sitting, do you default to folding your hands in your lap like a good girl? Hands folded in your lap will pull your arms in and your shoulders forward, making you contracted and closed. Remember that "contracted and closed" is a low-power position. Better to put your arms on the arms of the chair. Or if you're sitting at a desk or table, rest your hands there – but keep them apart, not clasped together.

Try standing up now, and stay away from what presentation skills coaches call "the fig leaf position" with your arms down and your hands clasped in front of you where a Greek statue's fig leaf would be. Again, clasping your hands will pull your shoulders in, making you contracted and closed. Instead, you might rest one hand on the back of a chair or the edge of a table. Even putting one hand on a hip can be helpful. Yes, body language coaches often recommend against putting your hands on your hips on the theory that it looks aggressive or scolding. But try it for now anyway. Your goal here is to take up space. To fully own the space you're occupying.

Just checking now: are your feet still flat on the floor? Many women have a habit of crossing one ankle over the other as they stand for any length of time; narrowing their base and making them wobble. That crossed-leg posture is seen as closed, maybe defensive, and can reflect a lack of confidence. Better to have your feet about hip-width apart, maybe with one slightly in front of the other, and both of them planted, drawing up that energy. Do you feel yourself shining?

Being Still

Now, as you settle into this confident posture, notice whether you have the urge to fidget. And resist that impulse.

There is something very powerful about stillness. Stillness radiates a calm confidence, a sense of command, contained energy. Stillness is magnetic. Conversely, when we see someone frequently adjusting their clothing, fiddling with their jewelry or touching their face, we know instinctively that they're uncomfortable or ill-at-ease. Shuffling the feet or shifting the weight from one foot to the other suggests nervousness. As much as we're drawn to stillness, we're put off by the aura of uneasiness.

I often see people stand up at networking events, ready to introduce themselves, but before they begin to speak they tug their sweater down, or pull at their skirt. Or they fiddle with their jacket. Or they flip their hair around or push it behind their ears. All that unnecessary activity distracts us from what the person wants us to pay attention to: their description of their product or service and what it can do for us. And the extraneous movements loudly signal their discomfort, which in turn makes their audience uncomfortable too.

If you're recognizing yourself in that description, don't feel alone. Most people have some nervous mannerisms to eliminate. Here's a story about mine …

When I was becoming a presentation skills trainer, learning the material we taught our clients, I got plenty of feedback from my new colleagues about what I was doing right and what I needed to work on. We also used video as a learning tool. And like most people; I wasn't that crazy about watching myself on a television screen. There was a lot to critique.

Among other things, I was horrified to see how often I touched my nose. I wasn't scratching it, exactly. It was just a light brush across the tip of my nose with the side of my index finger. Watching my videos, I saw that gesture again and again and again. It looked goofy, especially on fast-forward. Plus, I know that the experts in non-verbal communication say touching your nose is a non-conscious sign that you're lying. (There's a reason Pinocchio's nose grew longer when he told a lie.)

Now I knew for certain that I wasn't lying about anything. It wasn't even a matter of truth or lies; I was delivering valuable information that was part of a training program. But as I gave it further thought, it occurred to me that there might be something to this lying thing.

You see, I'd been in radio for 25 years; I surely knew what I was doing in that arena. I was well-regarded in the field. In fact, I was the sort of person young women, new in the business, called on for advice.

But radio was in the rearview mirror now. I was brand new to this business communication consulting firm; I was learning a ton of new material not only about presentation skills but also about business. The truth was that I had always been more of a performer than a business person. And now, here I was: I'd gone from being the seasoned, savvy broadcasting veteran to being the rookie consultant at my firm. I hadn't even done a presentation skills program for real clients yet. I definitely didn't feel like an expert. In fact, it would be fair to say that I felt like a fraud. And … I touched my nose. A lot.

There's physiology behind the assumption that nose-touching reflects lying. When we're anxious, the tiny capillaries in noses and ear lobes expand – you might know someone whose ears get red when he's on edge. That change in the capillaries produces a slight sensation, barely noticeable, maybe even below the conscious level. But there's that feeling, in our ears or our nose, and without paying much attention to it, we react by touching them. And to anyone who's paying attention to us, that reaction instantly reveals our inner discomfort.

There's nothing like seeing them on a video to make a person consciously aware of her quirks. Awareness was my first step to changing that nose-touching habit. It took considerable effort to keep my hands away from my face when I was in front of presentation skills training participants. It also took some practice. But as I got more comfortable in my new role, I felt less nervous, and also less inclined to brush my finger across my nose.

What about you? Do you have a characteristic nervous gesture? Holding your hand on your neck, maybe? That's a particularly vulnerable, low-power position. Scratching your head? Twisting your ring or rubbing your fingers together? Picking at your nails or cuticles? Please tell me you don't play with your hair! Hands-in-the-hair is a girlish mannerism that drains a woman's power faster than anything else. And it's very common.

Young women often have a hair-twirling habit left over from when they were eight. I've actually seen clients sit in a business meeting and twirl their hair; some of them use two hands to do it, as if they're braiding it. I'll never forget the brand new investment banker, deeply resentful of her perception that the men on her team didn't take her seriously. When I suggested that she might make a stronger impression if she didn't twirl her hair during a sales conversation, she had no idea what I was talking about. It was such an unconscious habit that she had to watch herself on video to believe that she still twirled her hair.

Most of us seem to outgrow the twirl as we get older. Instead we might fluff our hair or pat it, or push it behind our ears, even if it's already behind our ears. And it's true that there is a time when that unconscious preening might be useful.

Here's a hint: in birds, unconscious preening is part of a mating ritual. Seriously. A woman's magazine gave this suggestion for letting that guy in a bar or at a party know that you're interested in getting to know him better: when he's looking at you, they recommended, touch your jewelry and fluff your hair.

Which explains why fooling around with your hair is not at all helpful in a business context, doesn't it? At a non-conscious level, it sends entirely the wrong message about you and your intentions.

In general, and this is true for both men and women, keeping your hands well away from your face and your hair will help you project a more powerful presence. Our hands tend to go to our faces or heads when we're nervous and ill-at-ease. And we instinctively know that about each other – so when we see someone scratching their head or stroking their cheek, or yes, touching their nose, we interpret it to mean they're uncomfortable, self-conscious, ill-at-ease.

Action Steps

If you have a chance to see yourself on video, take advantage of it. You might be surprised at what you see, as I was when I watched myself touching my nose like that. Or ask for some feedback from someone who can see you more objectively than you see yourself. In some ways, that outside view can be even more helpful than a video. We're so used to our own way of being; we can watch ourselves on video and not even begin to notice habits that leap out at a more impartial observer.

Or we might see the action, but miss the significance of that characteristic gesture or posture – we see how we behave, but we don't interpret it from the inside the way others do when they see it from the outside. It's fascinating to find out what other people notice about your posture or gestures or the way you move.

Increasing your awareness will help you make the shift into your more confident, charismatic posture: grounded, centered, vertical, and in command of your space.

And once you're there, remember to BREATHE.

It might seem funny that I'm reminding you to breathe ... but the breath is actually a big part of projecting a powerful presence.

And people do sometimes stop breathing, temporarily. When I was sharing an office with a business partner, I noticed that she asked me often if something was wrong. "What's the matter?" "Are you okay?" "What's going on?"

I was perfectly fine – well, okay, not perfectly fine, but fine enough. I couldn't figure out why those questions kept coming up. Until I realized that my partner was hearing me sigh. And the reason I was sighing is that I had been unconsciously holding my breath. And the reason I had been holding my breath was – stress. Try it for yourself and see: if you hold your breath long enough, eventually you'll let it out with a sigh.

Think about what happens when a person is nervous or anxious. Their breathing becomes shallow and maybe rapid; and from the outside, we notice the tension. Tension is never charismatic. People are drawn to someone who seems relaxed and confident and comfortable in their own skin. A person who's tense or brittle has the opposite effect; we want to back away from them and not that slowly.

Sit for a minute now in your feet-on-the-floor, straight-spined, relaxed-shouldered posture. Breathe in through your nose, and breathe all the way into your core. So as you breathe in, you feel the expansion in your belly and your ribcage. But your shoulders don't move. There's none of that shoulder-raising that goes with shallow breathing. You're using your full lung capacity here.

Just let your breath find its own natural pace. It doesn't matter how fast or slow it is, although you may find that as you intentionally breathe into your core, you naturally breathe somewhat more slowly than is typical for you. As you continue to breathe consciously you'll notice your whole body relaxing. Muscles you weren't even aware of will begin to release. This should feel good. (And if you've skipped doing this, go back and read the last few paragraphs again and play along. It really will feel good.)

As your body relaxes and the oxygen flows freely, your magnetism increases. And the same thing will be true when you're not sitting alone with a book ... when you're in a social situation, or in a business setting. The energy that comes from really breathing fully will make you look more confident and charismatic.

And this may be the most important part about projecting a powerful personal presence. Remember that the nonverbal cues that tell other people you're confident and in command of yourself also tell you that you're confident and in command of yourself. This is an upward spiral: the more you look confident and in command ... the more you'll feel confident and in command.

CHAPTER 4
The Face of Confidence and Charisma

The Eyes Have It

When it comes to projecting a powerful presence, there's nothing more important than steady, direct eye contact.

If the people in my Professional Presence workshops are a good indicator, most folks think they do okay when it comes to eye contact. A good percentage of them are stunned, when we put it to the test, to discover that they're actually very uncomfortable meeting and holding someone's gaze; their eyes dart around frequently. And if they're in a situation where they have to meet with more than one person at a time, they have no earthly idea how to make eye contact work for them in a group situation.

What makes eye contact so important? In American business culture ... and it's important to say that the expectations are radically different in some other cultures ... but in American business culture, we associate direct eye contact with what? Honesty, confidence, and a genuine interest in the other person. And that's just for openers.

On the other hand, if I'm talking to you, but I'm looking off into the distance or glancing down at my shoes, you're liable to think I'm hiding something. Or maybe I'm insecure. Or I'd rather be talking to someone else. Or I'm just out-and-out lying to you.

So using eye contact well is an important skill to master. And like any other physical skill, it can be mastered. I'm very certain of this because I did it.

When my radio career caved in, you already know that I reinvented myself. It was by no means instantaneous – but I reinvented myself as a communication skills trainer and coach. The whole transition story is a subject for another book. But for now, you can join me (in your imagination) in a conference room in a New York office building, not far from Grand Central Terminal. There are maybe 10, 12 communication consultants in the room. And a few more in Toronto and Chicago ... they're joining us by way of one of those gray starfish-looking conference call phones in the middle of the table.

I have the next ten minutes to give what amounts to a sales presentation, which is something I have never done before in my life. Ten minutes to explain to these consultants why I would be a fabulous addition to their firm's Chicago office.

You can plainly see that I am quite nervous. This is a completely new situation for me. I've been out of work for nearly a year at this point; the money is gone and the debt is growing. And I'm finding that the funny thing about people who hire corporate trainers is ... they're not that interested in hiring someone who's never been a corporate trainer before.

There is a lot riding on the next ten minutes. They're going to hire me – or not – based on how this presentation goes.

Now that I think about it, this sounds a lot like the Trier Social Stress Test, doesn't it? And I'm afraid you don't have to look too closely to see the evidence of my stress.

There they are, these consultants, watching me; ready to jot down notes about me, evaluating me. So I start talking. And there's this woman over on my right – she is so warm and responsive, so nice, she's exactly the kind of person you'd want in an audience. And it's pretty easy to look at her sometimes as I talk.

And then there's another woman on my left who is obviously not digging my act. I can practically see the thought balloon over her head: what are we doing interviewing this radio chick? I can hardly stand to look at her at all; in fact, I'm desperate to avoid eye contact with her. And mostly I scan the room, because I know I'm supposed to be looking at somebody, right? I don't know much about sales presentations, but I do know you're supposed to make eye contact.

So … we can, mercifully, fast-forward to the end. They ask me a few questions and I answer them. Actually, that part is a little bit easier than the presentation. It's a little bit like having a press conference, and unlike sales presentations, press conferences are very familiar to me. I'm pleased that there are even some questions from the consultants in Toronto and Chicago.

Then the CEO says, "Why don't you go get a cup of coffee, Catherine, and give us a chance to talk about you?" As you might imagine, this is the most stressful Starbucks run I've ever made.

When I come back, they've designated one consultant to sit down and have a talk with me. And yes, he does make me an offer. (Hallelujah!) He also tells me the feedback from his colleagues was this: "She needs a lot of work on presentation skills. And what is her problem with eye contact?"

Here's the thing. I was in radio for 25 years. There's no eye contact there. I had no idea I even had a problem with eye contact. In fact, if you'd asked me about it, I would have said, "Sure, I'm completely comfortable looking people in the eye; I don't have any issues about that."

But the truth is, in this New York conference room, the people I made the best connection with … were the consultants in Toronto and Chicago. When I answered their questions, my eyes were locked on that gray, starfish-shaped phone in the middle of the conference table. Just the same way that, back in a radio studio, my eyes would have been locked on a blinking phone line. And even though the people on the phone couldn't see me, they could feel that connection, that energy.

Learning to be a business communication consultant, I had to practice a lot of delivery skills, but none took more effort for me than eye contact. Once they called it to my attention, I discovered that I did have issues about eye contact. I often talked to even close friends while looking off slightly to one side or down at the floor. And I also noticed that when conversations got particularly intimate, or I was talking about something that made me uneasy in any way, I looked off to the side or down at the floor even more.

Well you know what they say about practice. I wouldn't say it made me perfect, but I did get very good at maintaining eye contact even in the midst of difficult or awkward conversations. And you'd be hard-pressed to find a speaker who uses eye contact better from the front of a room.

Here's what you should take away from this story:

You may not know you have an eye contact problem. I had no idea it was an issue for me.

Whatever discomfort you feel looking someone in the eye, it will be aggravated in stressful situations. So you'll really have trouble with it in a job interview, a high-stakes sales meeting, a big presentation. Or a conversation about a subject you really don't want to talk about (and let's face it – sometimes we have to have those conversations).

Most interviewers or clients or audiences will never give you the kind of feedback those consultants gave me. They just won't hire you. Or they won't do business with you. Or they won't trust you. Because when you fail to make solid eye contact, they conclude that you are insecure, dishonest, uncertain of what you're saying, or … not really interested in what they're saying. And, it's important to note that they may not even be aware of exactly what gave them that impression. It's just a feeling they get. And people act on those feelings.

Eye contact is a physical skill; as with any other physical skill, you can get better with practice.

Action Steps

Practice.

And the time to practice is not when you're having one of those high stakes conversations. The time to practice is at dinner with your family. Or having coffee with a friend. Or when you're paying for your purchases at the drug store. When the stakes are low, when there's nothing riding on the outcome, that's when you practice making eye contact.

Now, it's not supposed to be a stare-down. You may run into somebody who is uncomfortable with eye contact – lots of people are. Of course you don't want to bore into them with your piercing gaze and make them uneasy. And individuals from some other cultures will have very different preferences about eye contact from Americans. So it only makes sense to accommodate those preferences.

The point is this: you want to make very sure that when you do look away it's genuinely because of the other person and their preferences, and not a reaction to any discomfort on your part. You want to get so comfortable with eye contact that it's under your control. That you choose when to look them in the eye, and when to look away briefly. That's very different from letting your eyes dart around because you feel uneasy.

As you begin to pay attention to eye contact, you'll probably notice a natural tendency to look away when you're thinking about the next thing to say. A typical pattern for right-handed people is to look up and to the left when they're reaching for a memory, up and to the right when they're imagining what something might look like sometime in the future. Ask someone about a feeling, and they'll likely look down toward their body. And people tend to look sideways, toward their ears, when they're trying to access the sound of something.

And because those eye movement patterns are natural, it's not necessarily wrong to look away when you're thinking. But there may be unintended consequences in a business conversation that make it worth practicing, so you can override the automatic impulse.

If you ask me what the investment will be for my Powerful Presence Coaching, and I look up at the ceiling before I give you an answer, your instant (and largely non-conscious) reaction might be: "That's not a firm fee." Or it could be: "She's not that confident about the value of the services she's offering." Or even: "I guess she's not really interested in me as a client."

None of those reactions are going to serve me well in our discussion, are they?

It is valuable beyond measure to be able to comfortably look someone straight in the eye, especially when you're speaking about issues that can be difficult or awkward:

- The price of your product or service

- The terms of an agreement

- Problems with delivering what you said you were going to deliver

- The salary you're seeking in a new position

- The salary you're offering to a prospective employee

- Anything else that puts a knot in your stomach

That's why we practice in those low-stakes conversations with friends and family and total strangers who don't have an impact on our future. We practice until we become so at ease with eye contact that we can continue to meet someone's gaze even when the stakes are high: when the topic is touchy, or when we expect to be challenged, or when we genuinely do have to stop and think before we respond.

Clients sometimes ask me if they can please, please, please just dodge the whole thing by looking at a person's forehead and faking eye contact. (Have you been sitting there wondering the same thing?)

Here's my response. When we talk about eye contact ... we're not just talking about your eyes. We're talking about contact. It's the contact that counts. So no, don't fake it. Go ahead and be brave and learn to create real contact with the people you talk to.

Because the magic happens when you have that genuine contact.

You radiate confidence. Your Presence grows. People respond to the connection you're creating with them even if they don't know exactly what they're responding to or why. Your personal magnetism increases dramatically.

AND, because you're putting your attention on them, whatever self-consciousness you may have felt will begin to diminish. I can get out of my own head and all the goofy things that could be going on in there (worry, distraction, regret, whatever) when I focus my attention on the other person or people. And eye contact may well be the best way to create that focus-on-the-other.

Bottom line ... when you get comfortable with eye contact you have an amazing communication tool at your disposal. You will feel more confident yourself, and other people will perceive that confidence.

A Smile is a Curve that Sets Everything Straight. Or Not...

While we're on the subject of your face, consider your lovely smile. Who knew that smiling could be so controversial?

Most of us would agree we'd much rather look at a smiling face than a sullen one or an angry one. We associate a smile with happiness, pleasure, a warm greeting, and more. So naturally, we're drawn to a person who smiles.

And we quickly distinguish one of those fake smiles that only involve the lips from a genuine one where the eyes crinkle and the inner corners of the eyebrows go down just a little bit. Even young children can tell the difference between real and phony smiles. Our innate ability to decode smiles might spell trouble for all those TV personalities and actors who've "had a little work done." Their puffy lips still smile, but their eyes can't. They wind up being very pretty, in a plastic-doll sort of way, but their charisma is impaired because they can't smile with their whole face anymore.

So a natural, felt smile conveys positive emotions, and we feel positive emotions when we see someone else smile, especially someone who's important to us. Research suggests the human brain actually recognizes happy faces faster, and from farther away, than faces that are reflecting negative feelings. We're wired to respond to the smiling face.

And there's some pressure on all of us to put on that happy face. Smile and the world smiles with you. Let a smile be your umbrella. You're never fully dressed without a smile. You get it.

But there's a catch in all this smile stuff for women. In workshops, I often tell the story of a trip to the grocery store one evening. I was in the check-out lane, my husband behind me putting the last of the groceries onto the conveyor belt while I waited to swipe my debit card. And then some random guy walked up to me and said, "Hey, you'd be so much prettier if you smiled."

Do you think that made me smile? It did not.

Here's the thing. I have never told that story without a roomful of women sharing similar tales of their own. It turns out that men will walk up to women in a hallway at the office, in a mass transit station, on the sidewalk, or just about anywhere else, it seems ... and say, "Smile!" Or "How come you're not smiling?" Or, "Put a smile on that pretty face." Or some other inane command to express a feeling that the woman in question may or may not in fact feel.

And guess what? Women resent it. Because the insistence that we smile implies that it is our job to be decorative. That it is our responsibility to make some casual acquaintance, or even a complete stranger, feel good. That we are not entitled to feel the way we feel, but instead are required to feel the way some guy thinks we should feel.

You'll notice that men never walk up to each other and say, "Smile, Dude." For that matter, women don't walk up to men and say, "Smile, Dude."

Because we don't expect them to be decorative. We don't think it's their responsibility to make a casual acquaintance or a complete stranger feel good. And we don't believe they're required to feel the way we think they should.

Here's a quick round-up of the research on men, women, and smiling.

Babies start smiling shortly after birth, but it's really random at first. Meaningful smiles start within a couple of months; that's when the baby starts smiling in response to some external stimulus like mommy's face, for instance. And yes, it's true. Baby girls smile more frequently than baby boys.

That continues throughout childhood – girls smile more often than boys do. Sugar and spice, and all that. Maybe you're familiar with the off-Broadway musical *I'm Getting My Act Together and Taking It on the Road*, which actually includes a song called, "Smile!" It begins, "Daddy always said I wasn't pretty unless I would smile. He said smile. So I smiled, smiled, smiled …" It's a girl's life, isn't it?

The gender differential peaks in adolescence and early adulthood. Some speculate that all those extra smiles on females are genetically programmed and have something to do with being at the ideal age (biologically speaking) for reproduction. The theory is that smiling makes a young woman more attractive and therefore more likely to draw her preferred mate.

As we age, the difference in smiliness diminishes but it doesn't disappear. All adults smile much less often than children do in an average day, but women continue to smile more frequently than men. Something like eight times as often in a typical day, according to some studies.

The gap between male and female smiling is greater in North America than in other parts of the world – we can only speculate about why that might be. And the difference in smile rates is bigger when people know they're being observed. When they don't realize they're being watched, there's not as much variance between the number of smiles seen on male and female faces. But it seems that when we know someone's watching, we're more likely to follow the gender-related rules.

In the corporate world, as women move up they smile less often; their daily smile rate gets much closer to that of their male peers. It's possible that the variance between genders at work has as much to do with occupation as with gender. Women are more likely than men to work in service positions where smiling is considered part of their job description.

When men and women are in similar positions, there's much less disparity in the frequency of smiles. Seems that women in higher positions feel less need to be decorative, to make everyone around them feel good, and so forth. Women with genuine power simply do not display those girlish grins.

What does all that mean for you? Well, it would be a drab world if we all stopped smiling, wouldn't it? So wiping that smile off your face is probably not the answer. But do start paying attention to your smile, and while you're at it, observe the people around you.

Action Steps

Notice when the women you know seem to smile just to ingratiate themselves with someone, or to reduce tension, or to appease somebody. Especially, watch the smiles that involve only the lips and not the rest of the face. Those are the unnatural smiles, pasted on for affect rather than arising out of genuine pleasure or amusement.

And notice when men do the same thing. You'll likely see a lot less of that.

Pay attention, too, to the responses you get in your business conversations. Is it possible that you're taken more seriously when you smile more selectively?

Make some notes for yourself about this real-world research you're doing. And know that it's perfectly okay not to smile.

On the other hand, if you want something to smile about, Google the phrase "men telling women to smile." You'll find some very entertaining essays about a cultural phenomenon that gets under a lot of women's skin.

CHAPTER 5
The Sound of Confidence and Charisma

And On That Note...

As important as your look is, people are also drawing conclusions about you from the way you sound. Not just the words you say, but the way you say them, the tone and pitch and pace of your voice. Do you say it like you mean it? Do you sound credible, knowledgeable, authoritative?

This is particularly an issue for women. You've probably had the experience of seeing a woman at a networking event, or in a sales meeting or a class ... she stands up to speak and she looks great. Professional, well put-together; nice outfit, great hair, even her shoes are right. Then she opens her mouth, and she sounds like a teenager, like, talking to her girlfriends at, y'know, the mall. And that perfect impression of professional polish falls apart. Her credibility plummets, her audience tunes out and she loses an opportunity to make a positive impression.

Let's look at some things that will help you make the most of your opportunities.

The Words You Speak

Crisp, direct language will serve you well. The more blah-blah you wrap around the point you're trying to make, the less likely it is that people will wade through it, struggling to understand what you're trying to tell them.

Notice whether you're in the habit of using runway phrases that don't add anything to your content. Beginning a thought with "Well ..." or "You know ..." or "Actually ..." or any other word or phrase that is not part of your content will diminish the impact of the words to come.

Even worse is the runway phrase that flat-out undercuts the message that's about to be delivered. And you hear these far more often from women than from men. For example: "This is only my opinion, but ..." "You've probably already thought about this, but just in case ..." "I'm not really an expert on this, but I just want to say ..."

Do you hear how that sets the listener up not to take you seriously? Many a woman has left a corporate meeting feeling that some guy just got the credit for her good idea. And very often, it's because she handed the credit to him when she prefaced her point with a phrase that negated its value. She all but told people not to put much stock in what she had to say.

You can begin to practice a new way of speaking now. Just start to say what you want to say ... by saying it! Straight out, with no padding before you get there. You'll notice that it's much easier to capture people's attention when all of your words have some actual meaning to them, even the very first ones.

How about hedging? You kinda, sorta, maybe say what you mean. Professionals who dilute their message with hedging words run the risk that nobody takes them seriously. Also – this stuff is contagious. I worked for a training manager who was notorious for sentences like, "I kinda want you to kinda get with

Becky and kinda go over the plan so we can kinda talk to the relationship managers and kinda ..."

Well, you get the picture. And because the boss talked that way, everybody on the team talked that way. No wonder we didn't have the impact on the organization that we would have liked to have! And it made our team meetings excruciating.

Listen to yourself on a recording, or get a friend to give you some feedback, or both. Is your speech sprinkled with "kinda," "sorta," or "maybe ..."? This is a habit you'll want to change in order to project a more powerful presence.

This is probably a good time to point out that gender differences in communication style are just that – differences. And there's considerable research about how they developed over many years and across cultures. There's nothing inherently wrong with women's way of speaking, in fact it has served us well in many contexts for generations.

The difficulty comes up in the business arena, where the male model of communication has been more prevalent. It's become the standard because for years, men were the ones doing business. We can bring our female sensibilities to the process, and it's probably advantageous for everyone when we do so.

But, we can also run into roadblocks because our speech is interpreted to mean something different than we intended. You may have read Deborah Tannen's classic books about male and female communication. (If not, I recommend them.) The first one was aptly titled *You Just Don't Understand*. The author was a guest on my talk show during her book tour – what a great opportunity to learn more about gender and speech.

Here's the gist of it. Dr. Tannen says, "Men grow up in a world in which a conversation is often a contest, either to achieve the upper hand or to prevent other people from pushing them around. For women, however, talking is often a way to exchange confirmation and support."

So historically, women's speech is more collaborative than men's. For example, we often ask tag questions at the end of a sentence to invite the other person's participation in the conversation. "This is a productive meeting, isn't it?" "She looks great today, doesn't she?" It's not that we don't really mean what we say; it's that we're interested in somebody else's opinion too. But, in a business setting, questioning what we just said can come out sounding wishy-washy or weak, or at least it can be interpreted that way by people who don't tend to use tag questions. Men, for instance.

Girls grow up being taught to be modest, not to brag ... and definitely to let the boy win. But it turns out we can carry that way too far and many of us do. Minimizing language is one of the ways we do that, playing down our strengths and abilities. Haven't you heard a female colleague refer to her "little project" or "a little presentation" or "having a little meeting"?

Another example of minimizing our work: using words like just or only. "I just want to say ..."

How can we expect anyone else to think our work is important when we speak about it in that kind of language?

On the subject of that need to play down our accomplishments...

Aren't You Lucky?

I learned a big lesson from a guest on my radio show, a woman maybe 15 years older than I was, and that much farther along in her career. During a commercial break, she was telling me about her experiences being interviewed on radio shows around the country, almost all of them hosted by men; she was curious about how I got where I was. "I've been very lucky," I told her. And did she ever stop me up short!

"You've been talented and smart and you've worked hard," she said. "Never attribute your success to mere luck."

Truth is, there's more to business success for any of us than talent, intelligence and hard work. Call it luck or fate or the Universe – there are outside forces that have an impact on us, right?

Opportunities seem to show up at the right time, people cross our paths when we need them, economic and social conditions change in our favor. All kinds of things happen in the world that help us along or put a gigantic roadblock smack in front of us.

But ... ask a man how he got where he is today. The first words out of his mouth are not likely to be, "I've been very lucky."

That is a peculiarly female thing, that willingness to attribute our wins to good fortune. Enjoy the good fortune for sure. But please, own your success – you earned it.

Who's Sorry Now?

Chronic apologizing is another habit of speech that gets in women's way. Some of us have said "I'm sorry" so often it's become an unconscious mechanism. I had a client who, at our first meeting, apologized for her hair, her outfit, her house, the dog, the kids, the traffic ... she must have said "I'm sorry" a dozen times in the first five minutes we were together.

Here's what's interesting – when I mentioned this rampant apologizing, she wasn't completely sure what I was talking about. But it became something to study. And what she discovered was that she did that all the time. At work, she'd often begin a conversation by saying, "I'm sorry ..." and then launch into whatever she was about to say. "I'm sorry" had become an automatic runway phrase for her, whether she was talking to the owner of the company or to one of her own direct reports. It wasn't about the other person's status or what they were doing or whether she was interrupting something; she just automatically opened conversations with "I'm sorry."

Listening to that, if we stop to think about it, we know that this very bright woman was not really apologizing for anything. "I'm sorry" is a vocal tic, like saying "y'know" or "like". But here's the thing. People don't stop to think about it. "I'm sorry" registers at the non-conscious level. And it makes the person who says it seem less important, or less worthy of time and attention, or just weak.

Once she became aware of what she was saying and the impact it was having, she stopped apologizing for every conversation she was about to have with anyone. And it made a noticeable difference in her relationships at work. In fact it wasn't long after that that she was promoted. And she was convinced her new title had everything to do with the stronger, more direct way she'd begun to communicate.

Many women develop a habit of apologizing with their tone, instead of with words. You might know someone – you might even *be* someone – who uses a tone of voice that sounds almost servile or groveling, sending the clear message that you don't really deserve someone's time or attention. Sound familiar?

A client called me not long ago, wanting to reschedule some sessions we'd planned to help her prepare for a series of presentations to potential referral sources. She began our conversation by saying in a high-pitched, childlike voice, "I've been very naughty. I haven't done my homework." So she's casting herself as the errant child and me as the mommy – and this has to stop. Because my assumption is that if she interacts with me that way, she interacts with other people in the same fashion. And that "I'm just a little girl" act will kill her professionally; nobody will trust their business and their money to someone who positions herself as a child.

I'll tell you how I stopped doing that sort of thing.

Years ago, when my nephew Kyle was maybe 4 years old, I took him to see David Copperfield at Chicago's Civic Opera House. I drove downtown in hideous Friday rush hour traffic, got to the general area of the Civic Opera House and then had no idea where to park or how to get there. I rarely found myself downtown in that after-work congestion – all those impatient, honking drivers, all those pedestrians marching toward the train stations and parking lots. All that noise.

So there was a cop trying to clear intersections and keep the traffic moving. I rolled down my window and told him, "I'm so lost. Can you tell me where's the best place to park, to come to the Opera House?"

The police officer gave me a suggestion. But it was Kyle who really made an impact. "Aunt Catherine," he said, "Why are you talking like a little girl?"

Why *was* I talking like a little girl? Because, I concluded, I was so uncomfortable making a direct request that I went right into this kind of phony pleading, slightly whiny, I-have-no-right-to-bother-you-but-please-help-me tone of voice.

And I realized that I did that a lot. Not just asking a police officer for directions, which if you think about it is an entirely reasonable thing to do and not something I needed to apologize for, with or without words. But often, instead of sounding like a competent adult asking an equal for assistance, I put myself in that one-down position with my voice, and probably with my facial expression too.

Kyle's question was a real eye-opener. I saw very clearly that I wasn't doing myself any favors with this shtick. And it wasn't fair to him, either.

Put yourself in Kyle's position for a moment. Here he is: a little kid from the suburbs, in a bustling, unfamiliar place ... gigantic buildings; honking cars; angry, tense people. But he's safe because he's with Aunt Catherine.

Except Aunt Catherine just evaporated before his very eyes and left a six-year-old girl in her place behind the wheel. Can you imagine how unsettling that must have been for him?

I learned a big lesson that day. I began to notice how often I talked in that I'm-so-much-less-important-than-you-are tone. And I made it my business to stop it.

These speech habits that make us seem so unsure of ourselves have an obvious negative effect on our business interactions. How can clients or customers or colleagues be confident in us if we're not confident in ourselves? But it goes way beyond that. They have an impact on the people who count on us to be in charge. Because they're counting on us, we need to sound like we're in charge.

Action Steps

If you apologize when you're not really sorry for anything or if you default to a little-girl voice that sounds like an apology without the words, now's the time to stop. If you hear yourself minimizing your work, or padding your statements with unnecessary words, you can let go of those habits now. They have been undermining your professional presence. You may find it helpful to do some work with a speech coach if you're not sure how to make these changes.

Are You Sure?

How many times have you heard a woman introduce herself in a sort of sing-song voice:

"My name is Catherine Johns? I'm a speaker and coach? I work with entrepreneurs and independent professionals who grow their business face-to-face?" And on and on, with a vocal question mark at the end of every sentence.

Linguists call that pattern a declarative with an interrogative intonation. It's a sentence that should have a period at the end of it, but the tonality turns that period into a question mark. And although you'll hear it now among young men as well as woman, it's historically a female speech pattern and it became rampant in the '80's as the language of the Valley Girl.

From a linguistic standpoint, it could almost make sense; it goes back to that collaborative impulse to include the other person in the conversation. A statement that sounds like a question is really just a non-verbal tag question, isn't it?

Here's the problem. Our tonality conveys meaning quite apart from the actual words we say. In American English, when the inflection at the end of the sentence stays flat, we hear it as a simple statement of fact. When the inflection goes down, we hear it as a command. And when the inflection at the end of the sentence goes up, we hear it as a question.

Let's say I tell you, "I hope you have that report finished." Depending on how I say the word "finished" it could come across as a bland statement of my desires; a strong hint that you'd better damn well have that report finished, and I mean it; or an innocent question about how far along you are on that report you've been working on.

When we say things that should be statements with that question mark in our voices, we communicate confusion, uncertainty, lack of confidence.

It's easy to imagine a business situation when we'd want to imply a question: maybe we're looking for more information, we want a client to expand on what was just said, or we're genuinely not sure about what we've heard and we're looking for some clarification.

But when we're discussing our services or products, when we're talking about ourselves and what we have to offer, when we're telling someone what we charge for the amazing work we do … that question mark creeping in is deadly. And when we're introducing ourselves … well, how can I possibly have any confidence in a woman who seems to be uncertain about her name and the name of her company?

The Pause That Refreshes

You know what's really powerful when it comes to the sound of your voice? No sound.

Yes, it's the pause that gives weight to your words. The pause is the white space that draws the listener's attention where you want it to go.

When you read a printed page like this one, you'd be looking at a bunch of black squiggles were it not for the spaces that break those squiggles into words and sentences and paragraphs. In the same way, when we listen to someone speaking, we need auditory spaces to make sense of what's being said. The pause gives our listeners a chance to understand and process what they're hearing.

The same way the mat around a framed painting draws the eye to the artwork, the pause gives emphasis to what we're about to say. And it makes what we're saying more attractive. The French composer Claude Debussy said, "Music is the space between the notes." Your speech becomes more musical when you include that space.

What gets in the way of the pause? Filler language: "um, uh, like, y'know, 'kay?" and all their cousins. Or sometimes you'll hear a person just draw out a wooooord, especially a word at the end of a phrase or sentence. They're extending the sound to avoid coming to a pause. And of course some people just keep talking reallyreallyreallyfast; that's another way to avoid that pause.

Truth is, most folks are uncomfortable with silence, even in small doses. Maybe we're afraid that if we pause we'll be interrupted, lose control of the conversational ball and never get it back. Maybe we don't really want to give our listeners a chance to absorb what we're saying because we're not that confident about our message. Maybe that incessant talking is just another way to discharge nervous energy, like tapping or fidgeting or pacing.

Presence happens in the pause, in that beat between thoughts. When you let your words breathe a little bit, you come across as comfortable and confident. You seem relaxed; that lets the people around you relax too and they will be much more open to what you're telling them.

Action Steps

Practice the pause. Listen to your voice recorded, or get a friend to give you some feedback. What are your habitual filler words? Begin to focus on eliminating them, so you have a bit of space between sentences. For most folks, it helps to slow down, too; rapid-fire speech will sound less confident than a more measured pace.

Speak From Your Core

A little-girl voice works beautifully for a handful of actors and comedians. Bernadette Peters, Kristin Chenoweth, Nancy Cartwright as the voice of Bart Simpson – these are women who've found fame and fortune with a cute or child-like voice.

For women in business, however, a lower, more resonant voice is an advantage, in part because it doesn't sound child-like. Most people find a lower pitch easier to hear and understand, not to mention more pleasant. And historically, roles of authority were almost always occupied by men, so humans have come to associate the male voice with authority. Beyond that, we've long associated a lower-pitched male voice with even more authority, possibly because it suggests more testosterone and therefore more dominance.

The famous orators of ancient Greece and Rome were men. The politicians famous for their stump speeches were, for generations, men. Modern technology brought us men as newsreel announcers, radio broadcasters, and later TV anchormen; even the commercials featured men telling us what do to.

That has equaled out a little bit now; there are far more women on the air in any of those roles now than there were even a decade or so ago. But the old prejudice remains firmly in place – the belief that people are more likely to follow directions from men than women.

And it pains me to admit that there's some substance behind the broadcasting business bias. Research does in fact show that both men and women are more likely to trust male voices than female voices. It's not much of a saving grace, but at least women don't distrust a female voice quite as *much* as men distrust a female voice.

Still, even comparing female voices to each other, a Stanford study found that people consistently perceived the woman with the deeper voice to be smarter, more authoritative, and more trustworthy than the woman who spoke in a higher pitch. People are more likely to dismiss information coming from a woman with a high, thin voice.

Early in her political career, Margaret Thatcher famously lowered the pitch of her voice with the help of coaching from Britain's National Theatre, arranged by the famous actor Sir Laurence Olivier. By all accounts, her new and improved speaking voice made a world of difference in the way she was perceived. And some of those accounts are distinctly unflattering. Thatcher's biographer Charles Moore wrote, "Soon the hectoring tones of the housewife gave way to softer notes and a smoothness that seldom cracked except under extreme provocation on the floor of the House of Commons."

The former Prime Minister demonstrated that it is possible, with the help of a professional voice coach, to measurably alter the pitch of your voice. For most of us though, it's not necessary to go to those lengths. What is helpful is to use the full range of your voice, and especially to draw on the lower end of your range, whatever your natural range happens to be. This lower end is the part that so many women don't use.

To draw on the full range of your voice, you need to speak from your core and not just from your head. When you hear a woman speak in a thin, reedy or nasal voice, it's coming from her head – it's a sound that can be piercing and unpleasant.

On the other hand, when the voice is fuller, rich and resonant, she's using what singers often refer to as the "chest voice" as distinguished from the "head voice." I call this speaking from the core. Of course to speak from your core, you must breathe from your core.

Think back to the breathing exercise you did awhile ago. In fact, this is a good time to do it again: Sit for a minute now with your feet on the floor, lightly pressing down. Your spine is vertical and your shoulders are relaxed. Let your head be aligned – straight up and down at the top of your neck in a neutral position. Breathe in through your nose, and breathe all the way into your core. So as you breathe in, you should feel the expansion in your belly and your ribcage. But your shoulders don't move up. Shoulder-raising goes with shallow breathing. When you use your full lung capacity, your shoulders remain still; the movement is lower in your torso.

It might take some practice to get into this rhythm where breathing in pushes your belly out. (Many people are in the habit of holding their stomachs in all the time!) It can help to put your hands on your belly, near your navel, and notice your hands moving in as you exhale and out as you inhale.

If you have a hard time with this, try the advanced abdominal breathing technique I learned from an actress. Stand up, bend over and plant your hands on your thighs, just above your knees. Now pant like a dog. Yes, it feels silly. Just give it a try. In this position, your belly will automatically move in and out as you pant, and you'll get very well acquainted with the sensation of abdominal breathing.

Okay, seated again, just let your breath find its own natural pace. It doesn't matter how fast or slow it is, although you may find that as you intentionally breathe into your core, your breathing naturally slows down a bit. As you continue to breathe consciously your body relaxes. Muscles throughout the body release and you tap into that good feeling of relaxation again.

And now we're going to take it even further, in the interest of enriching your voice. Relax your neck and throat. Release your jaw, so your lips may still be closed, but your teeth are slightly parted. Notice whether you've been holding tension in your jaw, as many people habitually do. You may even want to lightly massage those jaw muscles a little bit, to help them let go.

As your jaw loosens, relax your tongue. No, really. You might be surprised how much tongue-tension interferes with a rich, resonant voice. Let your tongue be loose on your lower palate, so you're using no effort there at all. Your tongue is just lying flat and broad on the bottom of your mouth.

Now yawn. If you're like most people, you're already yawning, just because you read the word "yawn." It's funny how contagious yawning is. But a good yawn or two will stretch your mouth and throat nicely and help you get warmed up for this exercise.

Next, as you breathe out, open your mouth, let your jaw be loose, and put some sound to the breath … a simple "Haaaaaaa" will do. Make sure your throat is open, your tongue relaxed, and the breath and the sound are coming from your core. If you put your hand on your chest, you should feel the resonance there.

You can experiment with different combinations of consonants and vowels. And vary the volume of your voice; notice that your abdominal breathing gives you the support to comfortably speak more loudly. You can shift from gentle to more forceful, increase and decrease the pace. Just play with your voice and notice the different sounds you can produce, staying with this voice that comes from the core.

The human voice is an amazing instrument; most people don't begin to take advantage of its full range. If you'll do these simple vocal exercises even for a few minutes a day, you'll find your voice will become fuller and richer. You'll easily be able to draw on the full range of your voice.

But when it comes to speaking from your core, I believe there's something else at work, beyond the physiology. I want to share something with you that's been very helpful for some of my clients.

Many women speak only with their head voice; they have trouble accessing a voice that comes from a deeper place in them; in fact, some of them have a hard time even understanding that a "voice from the core" exists, much less learning to use it.

I often suggest that they look at what might be blocking them from speaking their truth. Because they really are blocked. It's as if there's an energetic barrier between their head and their core. And that blockage often results from a lifetime of holding back, choking down, swallowing their words instead of putting those words out into the world.

It can be difficult to speak our truth, can't it? There's so much pressure on girls to be nice and agreeable and other-oriented, and that pressure doesn't really let up once we're adults. In fact, sometimes it intensifies. It comes from society, from families, from workplaces, and yes, sometimes we put that pressure on ourselves. We take on the job of making everyone else happy.

I argue that we pay a price for that in a lot of ways. And one of them is that we lose our authentic voice, so much so that even as full-grown adult women we continue to speak in a child's tone.

A workshop participant with a very high, tiny voice had a major "AHA" moment when I spoke about how often women squelch themselves, creating this barrier in the throat. She'd had an older sibling who had what we now call special needs. From the time she was a baby, this woman had been consistently told: "Be quiet." "Don't bother Mommy." "You can see I'm busy with your brother." "I can't listen to you now." And so on and so on.

Little wonder that she had learned early on to hold back, choke down, and swallow her words. She was the good girl who didn't demand, or even seem to need, much attention. There was a big block there for her. And that means there was also big opportunity to create a shift for herself.

Action Steps

There's only one action step to take here: start speaking your truth.

Of course we don't have to voice every thought that comes into our head. Some things really are best left unsaid, aren't they? But if you're like most people, there are times every day when you're inclined to speak up about something and in the end, you cave in and decide to keep it to yourself.

And if you're like most *women* there are a lot of those times. Maybe it's a conscious decision or as likely, it's just your habitual response to uncomfortable conversations. Either way, you find yourself holding back from saying what you mean to placate someone else, or to smooth things over, or to hide who you are and how you really feel. I'm proposing that you come out of hiding a little bit.

Once a day, when you notice that impulse to stifle yourself, resist it. Without any judgment. Just take a deep breath, sense your feet on the floor so you're grounded, get in touch with your solar plexus, and give voice to what you're really thinking, how you're really feeling.

Start with low-risk situations that won't endanger important relationships. This exercise in truth-speaking is like, well, like exercising a muscle. It's best to start small and work your way up as you get more comfortable. Give your honest opinion. Say no to a request instead of a grudging yes. Acknowledge how you actually feel. And as you remove that barrier, eventually you may want to take on the big stuff. Some women find that there are important people in their lives who have no idea how they really feel about things. It can be liberating, if a bit frightening, to let those people in.

Pay attention to what happens when you allow your authentic voice to emerge from your core. Making some notes for yourself may help you process this. How does it feel to you when you speak your truth? How do other people respond when you speak your truth?

Really looking at this issue can be deep work; you may want to find some support if you're inclined to take it on. And if even thinking about it makes you squeamish, that's a good hint that you probably should take it on.

We need to be very clear about one thing. The goal of all this work with the voice and language is not to turn ourselves into men.

The goal is to speak with the authority of a self-assured adult woman, and to eliminate habits that make us seem immature and uncertain of ourselves. This is about sounding confident and charismatic.

CHAPTER 6
Shine Like the Moon

Lighten Up

Up to now, we've been talking about how you can project confidence and charisma, as if it's all about what comes from you. But the truth is that charisma does not occur in a vacuum. Charisma has everything to do with the way you interact with others.

So you can walk into a gathering and sparkle, you can dazzle people, you can light up the room with your personality ... you can shine like the sun.

Or you might shine like the moon instead. The moon doesn't generate its own light; rather it reflects the light that comes to it from another source. But just think about all the songs and poems that have been written about that fabulous moonlight. When you reflect another person's light, you wind up shining brightly and beautifully.

There are some specific things you can do when you want to set other people up to shine.

Listen Up

A British woman in the 1800's is said to have commented on two great statesmen: "When I left the dining room after sitting next to Mr. Gladstone, I thought he was the cleverest man in England. But after dining with Mr. Disraeli, I thought I was the cleverest woman in England."

Brilliant men both, William Gladstone and Benjamin Disraeli. But which of them had greater charisma? They were competing to become prime minister; Disraeli won.

A key component of charisma is listening attentively, making someone feel that they are the most important person in the room (or the cleverest woman in England).

Now I typically work with clients who want to speak better, and there's a lot of demand for that. People want to discover how to craft a compelling message and deliver it with confidence and charisma. They understand how much it benefits them professionally to be able to speak well. But because communication is a two-way street, I also focus on listening. And I've pretty well concluded that most people don't really care about becoming better listeners. Although it would certainly be okay with them if the people around them listened better.

But that's short-sighted. Because no matter what you say or how you say it, the individuals you interact with – your clients, your colleagues, and certainly your friends and family – will think you are brilliant if you give them your attention.

People have this deep need to feel that somebody somewhere is listening to them. And if you're that person, they feel bonded to you, connected to you. That's good for your business of course. And it's good for human relationships, too.

When I was a talk show host, I used to say they should call it not a talk show but a listen show. Because the listening part was so much more challenging than the talking part. When I was a talk show host, I did an occasional segment called *Who Are You*. We'd start the show with that Who song, "Who Are You?" back before it became a TV show theme song. And the bit was this …

People would call in, and I would ask them a couple of questions. What were you like in fourth grade? What was the last movie you saw – in a theater? Do you believe in love at first sight? Tell me about your first date. What did you do in your first job? Who was the most influential person in your life – so far? These questions had nothing to do with their opinions about any of the burning issues of the day. These questions were designed to reveal – in the answer -- something about who they are.

So just for a minute, come with me into the studio – imagine a microphone in front of us. And on the console, there's a row of ten lights, one for each phone line. One of them is blinking slowly – that's the person who's on the air with us now. And the others are blinking very quickly – those are the nine people on hold, waiting for their turn to talk.

As soon as we say goodnight to the person who's been answering my questions, that line is empty and in a nanosecond it lights up again. Because somebody is sitting out there, somewhere in the Midwest, pressing redial over and over and over to get into this show. And we can see by the blinking lights that people are waiting and waiting and waiting to be on the air with me.

They're sitting through all the other callers. They're sitting through the seemingly endless commercials. They're sitting through the traffic and the weather and the network news at the top of the hour.

Now in talk radio, it's not that unusual for people to wait around for a long time for an opportunity to spew their opinions about whatever subject is on the table. The president is an idiot.

Congress is worse. And don't get me started on that lousy mayor. If you've ever listened to a radio talk show, you know that people love that stuff.

But this is a very different program. Consider this.

People are sitting on hold for an hour or more – and they don't even know what they're going to talk about, because they don't know what I'm going to ask them. People are sitting on hold for an hour or more because somebody is about to listen to them. And they desperately need that.

It is not uncommon for people to remember those shows even now, years later. They remember not because of anything I said, but because I listened to them. And because I listened to them, they feel a lasting relationship to me. Imagine how valuable would it be for you to create that kind of connection with your clients or your colleagues, or anyone else you interact with.

Now, of course I'm not the first person to figure out that listening is important. Even the U.S. government proclaims that listening is important. (Not that they do that much of it.)

The Department of Labor created the Secretary's Commission on Achieving Necessary Skills (SCANS) to come up with a list of foundation skills for the American workforce. And of course listening is a key skill on that list. If listening is a foundation skill for the entire American workforce, you know it's a critical skill for professionals who aspire to succeed, whatever business they might be in.

You may not know that there's actually an International Listening Association. You can even become a Certified Listening Professional. And get this – you'd have to take a year-long course to become a Certified Listening Professional! And the association warns in advance that it requires a serious commitment to the extensive work involved. All of us should probably do it. Because we will be better at our business, whatever our business is, when we become better listeners.

There are some steps you can take, though, short of signing up for a year of intensive training.

Seems to me, the first thing to do, if we want to be better at listening, is to acknowledge that it's not that easy. Listening doesn't just happen automatically. In fact, there are a lot of impediments to effective listening.

Some of those barriers to listening are environmental issues. Noise in the room, other conversations going on in our vicinity, or maybe if we're on the phone there's a bad connection. Can you hear me now? Well no ... as a matter of fact. There might be other kinds of distractions around us that interfere with our conversation.

Physical barriers can sometimes get in the way of listening. For openers, I could have a hearing impairment. People sometimes talk about hearing and listening as if they're the same thing. In fact, hearing is a physiological process. Sound waves hit the eardrum, produce vibrations ... and we hear. Or we don't. For some of us, the physical apparatus doesn't work the way it's supposed to, or perhaps the way it used to, and we don't hear as well.

But even if a person's hearing is fine, there might be other physical issues that interfere with listening, which is the process of making sense out of those vibrations. They could be cold ... or hungry ... or tired ... or they drank too much coffee and they need to excuse themselves. Any of those physical sensations that draw one's attention away from the conversation can interfere with listening.

And obviously, there are emotional barriers to listening. Just off the top, I might not like the person I'm trying to listen to and that makes listening tough. You know how that is, when you know you should pay attention, but you just don't like this person? In a perfect world, of course, we'd like all of our clients and our colleagues and everyone else we encounter in a day. But the world is far from perfect; some people can be quite unpleasant and some are fine people, but just not our cup of tea. And when we don't much like someone, it's a challenge to give them our full attention.

Or it's possible to have an emotional barrier to listening that has nothing at all to do with this individual. I could be angry about something that happened on my way to work this morning. I might be worried about something coming up later in the day. Or stressed about my growing to-do list. Or I could be sad about something that is completely unrelated to this person and this conversation. But, those powerful feelings can take my emotional energy away from listening here and now.

A huge barrier to listening is multi-tasking. That's why we have laws that prohibit driving and talking on the cell phone at the same time. Because it's dangerous.

We like to think that we can do two or three things at once and do them all well. Women, especially, often pride themselves on their ability to multi-task. But that's not really the way the brain operates. In fact, the human brain processes information sequentially rather than simultaneously. Our brain is actually wired to flip very quickly from the phone to the road and back again.

So it's common knowledge now that if we're yakking on the phone, our driving suffers. But guess what? So does our conversation.

A study at the University of Illinois found that driving during a conversation impairs a person's ability to comprehend and remember what they're hearing. Or, as Psychology Professor

Art Kramer put it, "Various aspects of language go to hell when you're driving."

If I'm talking to you and answering my email, I'm not doing either of those things as well as I would be if I were only doing one of them. When I worked at that business communication consulting firm, we had an unwritten anti-multi-tasking rule. If you stopped at my desk wanting to talk with me, and I was working on an email, I would either stop typing, look at you, and have a conversation … or I would say, "I can't talk right now, let me finish this and then we'll talk."

But we didn't try to do both things at the same time – because we knew that you can't. And the quality of relationships in that office reflected the intention to listen.

So if we acknowledge that all these things get in the way of listening … how do we set about to become better listeners? I'm going to offer some suggestions. And then I'm going to offer you a challenge as well.

If you want to listen better, the first thing to do is to set your intention to listen. Listening really is an act of will. It doesn't just happen automatically. Just because my lips are moving, it doesn't mean that you're listening to what's coming out of them. It takes a decision to listen.

And this might be obvious, but it's worth saying anyway. If I'm going to listen to you perhaps the very first thing I need to do is: stop talking. That's challenging for some people; especially those of us who are naturally gregarious. You know the old saying: You have two ears and one mouth so you can listen twice as much as you talk. And sales experts would mostly recommend that you listen three or four times as much as you talk. And then listen some more.

It's very easy to talk too much. We're enthusiastic about our work, we're enthusiastic about our products, and we're enthusiastic about what we can do for our clients. It's easy to just ... run off at the mouth. So, if I want to be a better listener, I need more economy in the way I express myself. I still need the enthusiasm, but I don't need so many words.

It helps, if you want to be a better listener, to face the person full-on. And think of yourself listening with your entire body. Of course we hear with our ears. But see if you can imagine yourself listening with the whole of you. As if you're a satellite dish receiving the signal. This full-body listening experience is much more powerful.

And looking at the person will help a lot. Then you can watch their physical cues as well as listening to their words. "Listening with your eyes" is useful because their body language supports and amplifies what they're saying. (Or sometimes it contradicts what they're saying, and that can be instructive too!) In any case, when I can watch the person, it helps me stay attentive to what they're saying; it also provides additional information through their non-verbal cues.

A client who's an audiologist tells me that a person's hearing begins to decline when they're still in their 30's. The stereotype is of older people being hard of hearing, but the truth is that our hearing begins to grow gradually less acute decades earlier. And we naturally compensate for that, without even realizing it, by reading lips. One consequence is that by late middle age, we find it harder to hear someone when we can't see their face. Knowing this, if our goal is better listening, we can intentionally capitalize on the tendency to read lips by making sure that we're looking at the person who's talking to us.

You might try increasing your listening ability by mirroring their body language just a little bit. Shift into their posture ... not in an obvious, phony way ... but leaning a bit the same way they're leaning, or tilting your head slightly in the same direction. Or if they're standing, you stand – if they're sitting you sit. Mirroring their posture will help you step into the reality of the other person. It's a way to put yourself in their place and that will help you listen more effectively.

Look for something about the person that you can like. Sometimes, I'll concede, this can be a stretch. But even in a person who's not your favorite, if you can find even one thing about them that's appealing or enjoyable or likeable ... it will be easier to give them your attention and listen to what they have to say.

Make it a point to listen all the way to the end of the person's sentence. Even when you are absolutely, positively certain that you know exactly what they're going to say. It can be so tempting – because we're in a hurry, because we want to move on already or maybe because we can hardly wait for our own chance to speak – to finish their sentence for them. And you know how irritating it is when people finish your sentences for you. Or when they just cut you off, and start talking before you've finished your thought. Yes, we all know, from experience, how irritating it is. So make sure you're not doing that to anyone else.

I've had a chance to practice that with a person who stutters. I found it extremely challenging to learn to wait and wait and wait ... and not to jump in and finish the sentence for him. I'd be thinking it's obvious where he's going, and can't we just get on with it and finish the conversation, this is taking too long ... but NO. I just had to stop myself from jumping in by sheer act of will. And sometimes I almost literally bit my tongue to do it.

But learning to be patient with him has been very helpful for me because it makes it so much easier to let other people finish their thoughts, and even to pause for a beat before I respond.

And there's another valuable hint there. That breathing room is so welcome; it's like a little oasis in the midst of a busy conversation-filled day. And the pause can also be a valuable information gathering tool. The truth is; most people aren't that comfortable with silence. So if they pause, and you don't jump in to fill that gap, they may very well fill that space themselves with information that you wouldn't have known to ask for. You can learn a lot about people by just pausing for a couple of seconds before you start talking.

When you're in the part of a sales conversation that many experts call probing (and wouldn't you think they'd find a less unpleasant name for that?) that extra bit of intel can make the difference between coming up with a targeted, responsive proposal that gets you the business and one that falls flat.

Giving people a chance to finish the entire sentence – and breathe – lets them feel that they have been heard. And they'll feel good about you as a result. Remember those talk show callers, and all they went through just to get that fabulous feeling.

Some people recommend that you sort of mentally restate what the person just said ... silently, in your own head. Here's why. Most people speak at a rate of somewhere around 150 words a minute, give or take. But we could listen to three times that much.

That means there's extra brain power available that isn't needed to track what your conversational partner is saying. And that can lead to the brain wandering off in any number of other directions. So it can help, when the person is pausing, gathering their thoughts, to mentally restate what they just said, as a technique to stay focused on the conversation.

It can be very interesting, just as an experiment, to imagine that I'm listening to this person for the first time. And this is especially helpful with people I've known for a long time. Because I think that I know exactly what they're going to say ... goodness knows,

I've heard it all before. (If this brings your spouse to mind, or maybe your mother, you're in good company!)

If I actually come to the conversation as if I'd never met them before, as if I'm hearing them speak for the very first time, it brings a freshness that can be fascinating. And I learn new things. And it stops my eyes from glazing over. Just try listening to one of the people in your life as if you've never heard them speak before and see how that goes for you.

You've probably run into suggestions, somewhere along the line, about active listening. Active listening is a communication technique that's been around for many years and a lot of people find it very helpful. The gist of active listening is: I repeat what I heard you say, in my own words. I hear it, I paraphrase, and I reflect it back in my own words, perhaps even incorporating the emotion that I think you're feeling about whatever you were saying.

And as I said, that can be very useful in a lot of ways. But I'm going to suggest a twist, because I think the "repeat it in my own words" part can put a person in the trick bag. The problem with paraphrasing is that I might actually be wrong about what I think I heard you say. As an example, suppose you tell me: "I really want to boost my business." And I say, "Great. I can help you get more clients." But it turns out you don't really want more clients. The truth is; you actually want fewer clients, but you want each one of those clients to pay you more money.

See, I said what I thought you said, but it wasn't what you really said. Or at least it wasn't what you really meant. That's the downside of active listening. Sometimes people end up feeling that that they weren't heard at all.

There's another way to approach active listening. Which is to repeat their exact words ... maybe with a little hint of a question mark in your voice?

I learned this technique, not as a business communication consultant, not even as a radio interviewer. No, I learned this technique as a nursing student. It's often difficult for people who know me now to picture this, but a long time ago in a galaxy far, far away, I was a nursing student. This turned out to be a case of serious miscasting, and I never did become a nurse.

But go with me, for now, and imagine me as a 19-year-old wanna-be nurse.

It's Nursing 101, the first class where we're actually in the hospital. Miss Mutke is my lab instructor, Miss Mutke doesn't like me, and the feeling is quite mutual.

Miss Mutke is explaining to us how to elicit information from a patient. And Miss Mutke is very clear that the correct way to elicit information from a patient is not to pepper the patient with a lot of questions. It's not to interrogate them about everything that's going on with them.

The correct way to elicit information from a patient is to ask one question, broad and open-ended. Such as, "How do you feel?" for instance.

And whatever the patient says, you repeat their exact words, maybe with a little question mark in your voice.

Well of course I think I know much better than Miss Mutke, and I say, "That seems silly."

She says: "Silly?"

"Well, yeah," I blather on, "you just want me to parrot what they say. I think that would be annoying."

"You think that would be annoying?"

"Yes, because they'll think I can't think of anything to say on my own."

"Oh ... you can't think of anything to say on your own."

By this time of course, everybody else in the lab group is laughing – they've already caught on that Miss Mutke has clearly demonstrated that this information-elicitation technique works. By using it on me! And I'm feeling more than a little foolish.

I took that lesson to heart, though. And I have found it so helpful. For years, I used it as a reporter and talk show host, getting people to open up and talk to me. And it's been just as useful to me as a consultant and businesswoman. Repeat their words. Their exact words ... with just the hint of a question mark in your voice. You can expect two results. You'll get high-quality information and you'll make a connection with them because they know that you listened to them.

People's exact words have a certain magic for them. When you use those words too, you tap into their magic.

What it comes down to, with every one of these strategies, is this: we get better at listening with practice. Listening is a skill and like any other skill, the only way to really get good at it is to do it.

So I'm going to challenge you to practice two things.

Action Steps

First, give yourself an assignment. Decide, let's say 3 times a day, you're going to really, deliberately listen to somebody. And you're going to use one of these techniques to do it. You can listen to somebody at home, or somebody at work ... or you can listen to the barista when you order your half-caf double latte. It doesn't matter who you choose.

Just pick somebody, and listen to them. And while you listen to them, sense your feet on the floor. When you're connected to your body, you're present, right? Our thoughts and our emotions can be in a thousand places at once. But our body can only be right here, right now. So be in your body, be present – and listen. And notice what kinds of shifts happen in those relationships and interactions.

And the second thing is this. Practice listening to YOU. Maybe this has happened to you. Not so long ago, my husband and I were having dinner, and I was going on and on about something that happened today. "Honey, will you pass the salt?"

I get the salt, shake it on, and I'm ready to resume the conversation. "Oh, what was I saying?" I interrupted myself … and then discovered that I didn't have a clue about what had been coming out of my own mouth 14 seconds ago.

Now that is a pitiful lack of attention. When I really listen to myself I am much more present. Not only present to myself, but present to the other person as well. So try listening to you, in that same intentional way … feet on the floor, grounded, centered, in your body.

And see what happens.

The Magic Words

Remember my nephew Kyle from an earlier chapter? He must have been all of three years old the day I arrived at his family's home and said, "Hey Kyle … whaddya say?" He scrunched up his little face and looked intensely thoughtful as he paused for a moment, and then took a stab at it: "Ummm … thank you?"

Like most children, Kyle had been taught those magic words, please and thank you, by grown-ups asking him, "What do you say?"

Okay, what do you say? Charismatic people are quick to thank others for their efforts, to acknowledge their contributions, to give them credit for their accomplishments. It's easy to take your colleagues and clients and service providers for granted; we get so rushed or distracted that we often neglect those magic words. But if you want to shine by letting other people shine, you can't beat "please" and especially "thank you."

My husband Frank is a genius at this appreciation thing. He not only thanks people directly in the moment; he acknowledges them to the individuals who make a difference in their lives. He's called the Walgreen's corporate office to let them know how helpful our neighborhood pharmacist was. He got in touch with the home office of Jewel to congratulate them on hiring such a good produce manager at our local grocery store. And I can't count how many restaurant managers have heard him rave about how terrific our server was that night.

The result? People think Frank is the nicest guy around and they can't wait to take care of him the next time he needs their help. Service providers get so used to being unappreciated, they absolutely glow when somebody acknowledges the work they do. This is another one of those upward spirals: when good service leads to praise it leads to even better service.

Look around you and you'll find people you do business with who need that affirmation that their work is appreciated. Express that appreciation and you really will think "thank you" is a magic word.

Action Steps

Thank three people today. Maybe it's someone who performs a service for you today, or maybe it's someone who makes an ongoing contribution that no one's mentioned for awhile. Either way, tell them what their efforts mean to you. And you get extra points if you follow Frank's lead and tell someone else whose opinion has a bearing on their professional life.

It's Complimentary

If "thank you" is good (and it is!) a genuine compliment is even better at bringing out the light in the people around you. People remember you for the feeling you create in them, and compliments make anyone feel good. It can be very useful when they associate that good feeling with you.

So you want to get busy and create some of those positive feelings; how will you go about it?

The most effective compliments are specific and personal. But beyond that, the subject of your praise can be just about anything. The work someone did on a newly completed project. An unusual piece of jewelry or a particularly attractive outfit. An insightful comment they made. A successful sales meeting. The possibilities are endless.

As much as people love a pat on the back, they're suspicious of anything that smacks of self-interest; they don't like blatant, phony flattery. So it's important to be sincere when you compliment an individual. Don't just make something up for the sake of handing them a bouquet; find something you can authentically appreciate about what they did or what they said or how they look.

Compliments are especially memorable when they come as a surprise. Like when Marv came up to me at the end of a recent meeting and raved about my new hairstyle. I was shocked that a man would even notice my haircut, more so that he commented on it; the exchange tickled me. Your unexpected positive comments will stay with somebody for a long time. And they'll generate positive feelings about you.

While we're on the subject of compliments, be very clear that confident, charismatic people don't just give them; they also know how to receive compliments graciously.

This is an issue for so many women. We hear that flattering phrase and we instantly dismiss it; worse yet, we often dismiss it out loud. Haven't you heard yourself saying things like "Oh, it was nothing." "I could have done better." "Well, it would look great if I were ten pounds thinner."

There are a couple of things wrong with those responses that downplay our strengths or our accomplishments. In the first place, if people hear us say often enough that we're not that talented or that smart or that attractive … they will believe us. We must know ourselves, right? They'll also take in our lack of confidence. Confidence is magnetic, it's an integral part of a powerful personal presence; when our confidence falters, we make ourselves seem small and insignificant.

Beyond that, remember that people associate you with the feelings you produce in them. How do you suppose it feels when you tell them they've made a mistake? And that's essentially what you do when someone admires you and you blow it off; it comes across as challenging their judgment or their taste or their discernment. You're basically saying they're wrong about you. And nobody really enjoys hearing that they're wrong.

Action Steps

Compliment somebody today. Keep an eye out for a reason to sincerely say, "You're terrific." Notice the response you get, the way a person lights up when they get that pat on the back. And pay attention to how it makes you feel, knowing that you've made someone feel as valued as they deserve to be.

The next time someone compliments you, remember those magic words. The appropriate response to a compliment is "Thank you." And then put your lips together and stop. Just stop. Don't dismiss it or downplay it or deny it, just thank the person and let yourself feel good about being admired.

And for a stretch, practice complimenting yourself. Yes, I'm serious. Stand in front of a mirror, look yourself in the eye, and tell yourself you have gorgeous hair. Or beautiful eyes. Or perfect lips. Or you did a brilliant job at work today. Or you're a great mother/daughter/wife/friend. Say it out loud. Say it like you mean it. And keep saying it until you do mean it.

I have a confession to make, and I'm putting this out there because I'm fairly certain I'm nowhere near alone in this. There was a time when I would often catch a glance at myself in the mirror and say mean, ugly things to myself. Things I would never dream of saying to another human being. And I'm not talking about a fleeting thought, briefly wishing I were younger or thinner or prettier. I would say mean things to myself *out loud.*

This is not healthy and it's not productive. It reinforces unpleasant feelings and it keeps a person stuck in negativity. That's why I've turned it upside down, and I'm suggesting you do the same.

Yes, complimenting yourself in the mirror will feel awkward. It may be quite challenging. Many women find this exercise brings up all kinds of emotion for them. Give it a try anyway; you'll find this experiment is an excellent way to get comfortable giving and receiving compliments, and it can be a huge confidence-booster too.

CHAPTER 7
A New State of Mind

Seeing Things

If you've taken the action steps suggested in these pages, you're already on your way to a much more powerful presence, and that aura of confidence and charisma will only get stronger as you continue to make these efforts. And yes, you *should* continue to make these efforts.

You've seen that changing your physiology will change your emotional state. You know that your body is a powerful tool, that you can literally change your feelings and your results when you change your physicality. As you experience more desirable outcomes over and over again, old habits will be transformed into new ones that serve you better.

As we wrap this up, you'll want to bring your mind into play as well, even more than you already have in some of the experiences suggested here.

You may be familiar with visualization, or maybe it's brand new to you. Now's a good time to begin using visualization to help you get into a confident, charismatic state, and stay there.

Why visualization? Performers, athletes and other high-achievers have long known the value of mental rehearsal or practice. It works nearly as well as actual rehearsal or practice because your non-conscious mind doesn't know the difference between reality and vivid imagination.

Try this out: imagine yourself holding a lemon. Notice how this lemon feels in your hand – the weight of it, the smooth and yet slightly dimply skin. Imagine yourself cutting into that lemon. You can smell the citrusy scent; feel the juice on your fingers. Now imagine taking a wedge of the lemon and putting it in your mouth. Bite into it and taste the juice as it squirts out into your mouth. If you're like most people, you're salivating right now. There's no lemon in your mouth, no citrusy scent, no juicy flesh. And yet, your body just responded as if the lemon were real.

The brain sends the same signals to your body in response to an imaginary situation as it does to the real thing. Repeated signals create neural networks. And thank goodness! Those networks or pathways keep us functioning in our daily lives without having to stop and ponder how to do everything we do.

When you're ready to drive somewhere, you don't have to actively think about starting the car; in fact it's likely that as you get in the car and head for work in the morning, your conscious mind is occupied with something else. But your brain signals your body to put your foot on the brake and press down just enough, turn the key or push the ignition button, check your mirrors, and put the car in gear. You've done it so many thousands of times, there's no need to consider each individual step. The neural pathways are already in place to take you from opening the car door to starting to drive.

You may not be aware of how deep those mental grooves are until you rent a car, or borrow one, or buy a new one. Then it's a surprise when your hand automatically reaches to turn the key, before you remember that this car has a push-button ignition. Or you start to shift into reverse and find that the gearshift handle is in an entirely different place than it was in your other car. To say nothing of turning on the radio or the windshield wipers! But as you drive it a few more times, new neural pathways begin to form, and it becomes natural and automatic to start *this* car and begin to drive.

That's exactly how visualization works. It creates new neural connections that can replace the old ones and lead to the results we want.

Basketball players have upped their free throw points by sitting on the bench imagining themselves making a basket. Golfers improve their scores by visualizing the shot in rich detail before they take it. Pianists play the music in their minds and find that when they sit down at the real piano, they play better.

And you? You can use visualization to rewire your brain, creating confidence and fostering success.

Here's how.

- Most people find it easier to make a detailed mental image when they close their eyes. As you get more practice at this, you'll be able to visualize eyes-wide-open, but for now, sit in a comfortable place and close your eyes.

- Allow your body to relax – let your shoulders drop, release your jaw, breathe fully and deeply.

- Remember a time when you were successful, even triumphant. You may access the same memory of confidence that you worked with at the beginning of this book, or you might select a different experience this time.

- Now imagine that scene playing out in front of you, as if you're watching a movie of yourself winning, succeeding, or getting the prize.

- You'll want your Success Scene to fill your whole field of vision, as if you're watching it on a gigantic theater screen, not your iPhone. Make sure it's in color, and make it as detailed as possible.

- Who do you see, in addition to yourself? What is everyone wearing? Are you indoors or outside? Fill in the details of the environment: colors, shapes, textures, everything you would be seeing if you were actually there in that situation where you were triumphant.

- If you're one of those people who say, "I can't visualize. I close my eyes, but I don't see any pictures" … not to worry. Imagine that your mental movie is playing on the other side of a heavy, velvet curtain. You can't see it, but you know for certain that it's there. (This is how I did it in the beginning, and with practice the mental pictures showed up.)

- Add sound to your mental movie. What are people saying? Do you hear applause, or people congratulating you, telling you how well you did? Are there other sounds around you?

- You might take a few moments to enjoy this; it's fun watching yourself do so well.

- **Now step into that scenario.**

- You're no longer watching it unfold in front of you; now you're living it.

- See everything you would be seeing through your own eyes: the people, the environment, even looking down at your own hands or feet.

- Hear the voices and any other sounds.

- Feel your feet on the floor or the ground. Sense the handshakes or high-fives or pats on the back. Feel the smile on your face and the crinkling around your eyes as you manifest your excitement about what you've achieved.

- You may even be able to smell something in the environment, depending on where your Success Scene is happening; flowers or food or even the sweat from a hard-fought athletic contest.

- Focus now on the *internal* feeling, and I don't know exactly what that feels like to you, but you know. So go ahead now and experience that whatever-it-is: elation, joy, happiness, confidence, thrill, excitement, warmth, triumph, delight, jubilation …

- Stay with that feeling for a moment. Enjoy it. And know that you have the power and the ability to recreate it anytime you want.

If you'd find it easier to hear the directions, rather than reading them, you can download an audio version of the visualization, with my compliments: www.showupandshinebook.com.

The first time you try this creative visualization, you may experience extraordinary results. Or you might need to practice a few times to develop a knack for it. Once it comes naturally to you to recreate a real-life situation, you can try visualizing something that hasn't in fact happened.

Use the same technique to imagine yourself knocking it out of the park when you do your next presentation. Or comfortably sailing through a sales conversation that might have seemed difficult in the past. Or wowing 'em in a job interview.

Whatever the situation, make a mental movie of it. Make your movie as richly detailed as you possibly can. The more vivid it is the better. Then step into the image (this is called associating) so you're seeing the scene through your own eyes, hearing it through your own ears, feeling what you would be feeling in the moment.

Make the climax of your mental movie the best possible outcome for you. And use this rehearsal-in-your-mind several times. Then use it several more. This visualization will be especially useful for you if you're in the habit of considering worst case scenarios or replaying your failures and embarrassments over and over and over. (Not that I have any first-hand experience with that, she said tongue-in-cheek.)

You're using creative visualization now to rewire your brain. In the past you might have defaulted to dark thoughts, anticipating negative results even before they happen, generating nervousness and insecurity. You're creating a new pathway here, a neural network that takes you to a brighter place and a better outcome. As you imagine yourself achieving your goal, you create confidence and a more powerful presence.

There's one more mental exercise you may find helpful as you develop your Presence. This has to do with getting present, here and now. And you can do it anywhere at any time.

Most of us have somewhere around 70,000 thoughts a day. And the vast majority of those thoughts are not original. We thought the same thing yesterday and the day before and last Tuesday and three months ago and … well, you get the idea. Furthermore, for most people, a huge percentage of those repetitive thoughts are negative or self-critical. (You didn't think you were the only one, did you?)

Honest self-examination can be helpful in many ways; if we act on it we can change our relationships, our careers and our very lives. But random thoughts about our lack of prowess, a physical trait we dislike, a mistake we made … these are not only not helpful, they're damaging. We rehash old experiences and feelings and doubts. And they take us straight out of the present and into the past where we marinate in a stew of regret, embarrassment and shame. Or they propel us into the future on the wings of worry, apprehension and fear.

We can develop our Presence by coming back to here and now.

- Breathe – and pay attention to your breath.

- Tune into your environment. Look around you and take note of objects, spaces, walls, light, and shadow. Really examine the space you're in and as you do, notice especially what you had not noticed before. Listen closely as sounds come into your consciousness, sounds that were there all along but outside your awareness.

- Tune into your body. Pay attention to the external sensations – where your feet touch the floor, where your body connects with furniture, the texture and weight of your clothing, the temperature of the air on your skin. And notice internal sensations too. Your breathing, your heartbeat, the clenching and relaxing of muscles.

- Say to yourself, out loud if you like, "I'm here, now."

- With your attention fully engaged in your surroundings and your Self, you've likely found that the background noise of mental chatter has evaporated and you really are here, now.

But the mind doesn't stay silent for long. When the chatter that the Buddhists call "monkey mind" returns (and it will) just do it all again. "I'm here, now." When you're here, now you have presence. You show up … and shine.

THE END

— except it isn't the end, of course. This is actually just the beginning.

If you'll follow the suggestions you've read here, putting them into practice again and again, you'll get more comfortable in your own skin, and that will make you more charismatic. You'll feel more confident about your future. And you'll be more at ease in challenging situations, because you have new skills to draw on.

If you stick the book on a shelf and skip the practice, you can't expect much. But if you play full-out you will develop the powerful personal presence that allows you to shine in business and social situations.

I hope you'll share your experience with me. It would be delightful to tell your story in my next book. You can get in touch at www.ShowUpandShineBook.com, or www.facebook.com/CatherineJohnsChicago.

ABOUT THE AUTHOR

Catherine Johns works with entrepreneurs and professionals who build their business face-to-face. Whether that means networking, speaking engagements, sales presentations, or all of the above, Catherine helps her clients get more magnetic so they attract more business.

Midwesterners remember Catherine from Chicago radio – as a news anchor and reporter, talk show host, and morning show side-chick at WLS and later at WJMK-fm. She learned to tell a story, engage an audience, and dance with the unexpected while working alongside legends like Larry Lujack, Fred Winston, and John Landecker.

Moving into the business world, Catherine became a communication skills coach and trainer, helping professionals capture the attention of an audience, be it seven people or 700. In addition to individual coaching, Catherine offers *Speak for Success* Workshops and keynotes. She gets rave reviews speaking to business groups, professional associations, and women's organizations.

Whatever the format or forum, Catherine's committed to helping professionals develop their personal presence, change the way they come across in business situations ... and improve the results they get.

Learn more at www.CatherineJohns.com.

CPSIA information can be obtained
at www.ICGtesting.com
Printed in the USA
FFOW01n1405210816
26933FF

9 780989 618700